ASTRONOMY

A FIRST BOOK

ASTRONOMY

FROM COPERNICUS
TO THE
SPACE TELESCOPE

CHRISTOPHER
LAMPTON

FRANKLIN WATTS
NEW YORK • LONDON • TORONTO
SYDNEY • 1987

Diagrams by Vantage Art, Inc.

Photographs courtesy of: Dennis Milon: p. 8;
Lick Observatory Photo: pp. 15, 18, 72;
The Bettmann Archive: pp. 32, 43, 54, 79;
AP/Wide World: p. 51; NASA: pp. 56, 86;
Harvard College Observatory: p. 68;
The Archives, California Institute of
Technology: p. 71; reproduced with
permission of AT&T Corporate Archive: p. 76.

Library of Congress Cataloging-in-Publication Data

Lampton, Christopher.
Astronomy.

(A First Book)
Includes index.
Summary: Surveys the history of discoveries and
theories in astronomy and the scientists responsible
for them, from Aristotle and Copernicus to Einstein.
1. Astronomy—Juvenile literature. [1. Astronomy]
I. Title.
QB46.L28 1987   520   86-23436
ISBN 0-531-10300-5

CONTENTS

ASTRONOMY

INTRODUCTION

SCIENCE LOOKS
TO THE STARS

Astronomy is the science that studies the universe of which the planet Earth is part. Scientists who practice astronomy are called astronomers. Astronomers have two jobs, really. One is to look at what is going on in the sky, using special instruments and making careful measurements of what they see. This may sound a little boring, and sometimes it is, but it has to be done if we are ever to know what lies beyond our planet, in the vast reaches of outer space. An astronomer who examines the sky and measures what is found there is called an *observational astronomer*, because he or she makes many observations of the sky.

The second job of the astronomer is to look at the measurements made by the observational astronomer and decide what they mean. An astronomer who does this is called a *theoretical astronomer,* because he or she creates theories based on the work of the observational astronomer. A theory is simply an explanation that makes sense of observations and allows astronomers to predict the results of future observations. This may also sound a little dull, but it really isn't. The theoretical astronomer can dream up wild ideas, like exploding stars and black holes, as long as these wild ideas agree with the observations made by the observational astronomer.

Of course, most astronomers are both observational and theoretical astronomers, since it's impossible to make observations without trying to figure out what those observations mean. When a scientist tries to figure out what a set of observations means, he or she invents theories to explain the observations. And once an astronomer has invented a theory, he or she must then make more observations to see if they prove or disprove that theory.

This game of theories and observations has been going on for a long time. Astronomy may be the oldest of all sciences, dating back to a time when people lived in caves. We know a lot more about the universe now than the cave dwellers did, though we are still a long way from knowing everything there is to know about the universe around us.

In this book, we'll talk about the observations that astronomers have made through the ages. More important, we'll talk about the guesses that astronomers have made as to what these observations meant. Some of these theories were wrong, but that doesn't make them any less important. In fact, it is these wrong guesses that led, over thousands of years, to the guesses that astronomers are making today. And even today there is a lot of argument over which guesses are right and which guesses are wrong.

When astronomers make a guess about what their observations mean, we say that they are creating a *model* of the universe, or of some part of the universe—the way that you might make a model of an airplane out of plastic parts. However, aside from the fact that the astronomer uses numbers and diagrams on paper to make a model of the universe, while you use glue and plastic to make a model of an airplane, there is an important difference between these two kinds of models. If you want to find out whether your model looks like a real airplane, you need only go to an airport or a flight museum to compare it with the real thing. The astronomer, on the other hand, has no way to compare a model of the universe with the real thing—except by observations made through special instruments. And that's not quite the same thing.

For this reason, astronomers are always changing their models of the universe, sometimes in big ways, sometimes just in tiny details. In the chapters that follow, we'll look at a lot of different models of the universe, and the way that they have changed over the years. Some of these models will seem quaint and a little funny. Others may seem too incredible to be true.

Which model is the correct one? Maybe we'll never know. But the fun in astronomy isn't always in *knowing* what's true but in *figuring out* what's true. As long as astronomers have things left to figure out, astronomy will be one of the most exciting sciences around.

THE ANCIENT
ASTRONOMERS

The stars have always been with us. Primitive human beings looked up at the sky and saw pretty much what we see today. At night they saw a sky rich with stars. Among those stars moved other bright objects, such as the moon and the planets. During the day, these objects were lost in the powerful glow of another object, called the sun.

The first astronomers—that is, the first human beings who looked at the sky and wondered about the universe that lay beyond Earth—must have lived thousands of years ago. Probably they lived before the dawn of written history, so we know nothing today of what they thought, or what they believed the universe was really like.

Today, we know a lot more about the universe than these ancient astronomers knew. And yet it's not hard to guess at what they believed and felt when they looked at the sky. You need only to step out of your house on a dark night and look up in order to experience the awe that ancient humans must have felt when they observed the heavens.

IMAGINE YOU LIVED
THOUSANDS OF YEARS AGO

Let's try a thought experiment, an experiment that takes place only in our brains. First, step outside your house on a dark night, as we suggested in the last paragraph. (Since this is a thought experiment, you don't really have to step outside your house on a dark night. That would make it difficult to read the pages of this book. You can just *imagine* that you've stepped outside your house.)

Forget everything that you may have learned about the stars and planets. Forget that Earth is round, or that space ships have traveled to the moon and beyond. Imagine that you are a person living a thousand years ago, pausing for a moment outside your mud hut after a difficult day of toiling in the fields. You are tired and ready for a long night's sleep, but for just a moment you pause to survey the world around you. In the distance, you see dark fields and forests and perhaps the fires of neighboring villages. Beyond the fires lies the horizon, a sharp line separating Earth from the sky, though barely visible now in the darkness. Above the horizon is the dark sky itself, punctuated by thousands of tiny pinpoints of light. In the middle of that sky hangs a great circle of silver, with dark markings on its face. This circle is not as bright as the sun that shines in the daytime sky, but it is bright enough to cast a haunting illumination on your hut and the dirt path that leads to it.

Suddenly you are overwhelmed by curiosity. You have known the night sky all of your life, since you were a toddling child. The elders of the village have told you that the sky is the domain of powerful gods, but this does little to answer the questions in your heart. What is the world in the sky like? What sort of gods inhabit it? Do the gods live in the shining silver orb above your head? Or do they live in the stars, or in the sun? How far above your head is the shining silver orb? If you stood atop a tall tree, could you touch it with your hand? You've never heard of anyone doing such a thing, but has anyone ever tried?

A star cluster

And what of the world on which you live? What is the world like beyond your village? How big is it? What sort of shape does it have? You have never been more than a mile outside your village, but you know of others who have gone farther. Surely, then, the world must be larger than a mile, perhaps larger than several miles.

Caught up in your thoughts, you have now forgotten just how tired you are. Without realizing just what it is that you are doing, you begin to speculate, to imagine the true nature of things you actually know very little about. You do not know what a theory is, and yet you start to invent theories about the world on which you live and the universe around it. You start to invent a model of the universe.

A MODEL OF
THE UNIVERSE

It is obvious, you think, that the world is flat. Your powers of observation tell you that much. You can *see* that the world is flat, all the way to the horizon.

And how big is the world? Well, it must certainly stretch all the way to the horizon, which looks to be a considerable distance, perhaps several miles. Could it stretch beyond the horizon? That's certainly possible, though you are less sure. Yes, you decide, it could stretch for quite a distance beyond the horizon. How far beyond the horizon? Well, it could stretch for many, many miles beyond the horizon. In fact, you have heard stories of distant villages that almost certainly lie a goodly distance beyond the horizon. Is it possible, then, that the world has no end at all, that it stretches beyond the horizon forever?

This thought frightens you. It is one thing to suspect that the world stretches for many miles beyond the horizon, another thing altogether to suggest that it has no end. No, that is too much to consider. The world must have an end. There must be some kind of border beyond which the world does not continue.

But if there is a border at the end of the world, what lies beyond that border? Nothing at all? Empty space? But if there is empty space beyond the border, where does the empty space end? Does the empty space stretch on forever?

This thought also frightens you, and so you turn your attention to the sky above you. Unlike the edge of the world, you can see the limits of the sky. The sky, obviously, is a black dome over your head. In some ways, it is like the roof of your hut, though much larger. This thought comforts you. Roofs are something that you understand. Of course, the sky is a very odd roof. For one thing, it moves. As the night goes on, the sky changes, as though it were slowly turning.

You can tell that the sky is turning because you can see many tiny lights placed inside the dome of the sky. Perhaps these lights are lanterns, like the burning fires that the village elders hang from poles during festivals. Or maybe they are holes in the dome, letting in light from beyond.

But if there is a light beyond the dome of the sky, then you cannot see the limits of the heavens after all. There must be something beyond the dome. And if there is something beyond the dome . . . perhaps it goes on forever, just like the empty space beyond the border of the world.

This thought frightens you again, and you decide that you have had enough speculation for one night. And yet, even as you enter your hut for a long night's sleep, you know that you will return to your study of the sky on another evening. Perhaps then the idea of a universe that goes on forever will not seem quite so frightening, and you will have some new thoughts about the world and the sky. . . .

WHAT YOU ACTUALLY SAW

It is safe to guess that you would have returned to your observation of the sky on many later nights. We have only to look at the sky to know what you would have observed. For instance:

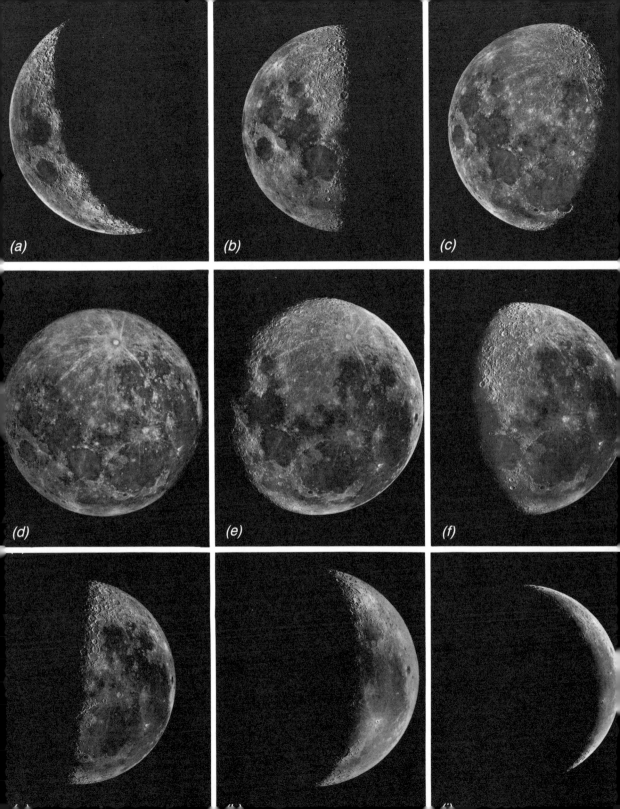

(a)

You would have seen the stars, the bright "lanterns" hanging inside the dome of the sky. As the sky "turned" during the night, the stars would have turned with it, as though they were permanently fixed inside the dome. With time, however, you would notice that different stars are visible in the night sky at different times of the year—that is, during different seasons. The night skies in the cold months of winter feature different stars from those of the night skies of summer, though the same stars invariably return each winter and summer.

You would have seen the planets. These pinpoints of light look like very bright stars, but they move differently. During the course of the night they move with the stars, but during the course of the year they follow their own paths. A planet that rises on winter evenings one year might rise on summer evenings the next. The very word *planet*, in fact, comes from a Greek word meaning "wanderer." There would have been five planets visible to your naked eyes, the ones we refer to today as Mercury, Venus, Mars, Jupiter, and Saturn.

You would have seen the moon, the shining orb that hung above your head on the night of your first observations. The moon also wanders among the stars, so you might have considered it to be a planet as well, though it is much larger and brighter than the other planets. It also moves faster. Though it would pass through the sky in a single evening much as the other planets and stars do, it would rise later every evening, appearing in a different place among the stars each night. It takes the moon almost twen-

The phases of the moon: (a) four days,
(b) seven days—first quarter, (c) ten days,
(d) fourteen days—full, (e) seventeen
days, (f) twenty days, (g) twenty-two
days—last quarter, (h) twenty-four days,
(i) twenty-six days

ty-eight days to travel completely through the stars, returning to the same position that it had occupied twenty-eight days earlier. The moon also passes through a series of phases, as it seems to disappear, then reappear a little bit at a time, then gradually disappear again. It takes the moon thirty days to pass through these phases. This is why even today we refer to a thirty-day period as a *month,* a word derived from an earlier form of the word *moon,* although today not all months are exactly thirty days in length.

During the day, you would see the sun. Although the sun seems to hang alone in the sky, with no stars or planets around it, you might have guessed that there were indeed stars behind the sun in the daytime sky but that you could not see them because of the bright glare of the sun itself. Today we know that this is true. And once you had guessed this, you would also realize that the sun moves through the stars day by day just as the moon does, though it takes a much longer time for the sun to make a complete trip through the heavens. Today we know that this trip takes roughly 365.25 days, and we call this period a year. (The extra quarter day is why we add an extra day every leap year.)

In a lifetime of observing, you might also have been lucky enough to see a comet, a starlike object trailing a bright tail behind it. Although it would have moved through the stars much as the planets and the moon do, the comet would not return year after year. Rather, it would disappear altogether after a few weeks of passing through the sky. (Actually, some comets *do* return after many years, but you wouldn't notice this.)

What would you make of all this? What sort of model of the universe would you invent to explain all of these observations? Maybe you would have invented no model at all; perhaps your curiosity would end at simply noting the movements of the stars and planets. But humans have always been curious creatures, and so you probably would have made guesses about great revolving spheres in the sky, or strange glowing creatures that flew in circles through the night. Almost certainly these theories, these models of the universe, would bear little resemblance to the theories of modern astronomers. This isn't because modern astronomers are smarter than our imaginary villager but because they have some pretty powerful advantages. They have telescopes that draw in light from the stars, and they can even launch rockets to travel among the planets and send back messages describing what they see. And they are able to build on the observations of thousands of curious men and women who have looked to the skies since the time of our villager. As the great scientist Sir Isaac Newton once said, "If I have seen farther than other men, it is because I have stood on the shoulders of giants."

Because the skies are the same now as they were in the time of our villager, you can go out into your own yard for real—not just in a thought experiment—and observe the skies and invent your own theories about the universe.

But before you do, you might want to read the rest of this book—where we will show you how astronomers over the last several thousand years have slowly built up a detailed model of what they believe the universe is like, a model that holds some surprises that would seem more appropriate in a science fiction story than in the sober pages of a scientific journal.

2

THE
GREEK VIEW
OF THE
UNIVERSE

Nearly twenty-five hundred years ago, a marvelous thing happened. A civilization of people arose on the balmy shores of the Mediterranean Sea who believed that it was possible for the human mind to grasp the secrets of the universe through the power of sheer thought. These people were the ancient Greeks.

This, as far as we know, was something completely new in history. Earlier peoples had felt that it was necessary to explain the heavens and Earth by saying that they were created by mystical gods, or that there were some things forever beyond the ability of people to understand. The Greeks, on the other hand, believed that human beings could uncover the secrets of the universe by thinking profound thoughts about them—or at least many Greeks believed this.

For instance, the astronomer Eratosthenes (276–196 B.C.) not only realized that Earth was round—other observers had already suggested this possibility—but he measured its size with incredible accuracy.

How did Eratosthenes perform this feat? Well, he lived in the city of Alexandria, and he had heard that at noon in the distant town of Syene, the sun cast no shadow. This meant that the sun was directly overhead at noon in Syene. In Alexandria, however, the sun did cast a shadow at noon, which meant that the sun's rays were striking the ground at a different angle there; hence, the surface of Earth must be curved. By measuring the length of the shadow of a stick at noon in Alexandria, Eratosthenes calculated the difference in the angle of the sun's rays. Then, using the north-south distance between Syene and Alexandria, he figured out the exact curvature of Earth's surface. By assuming that Earth was a perfect sphere or globe—which it isn't, but his guess was close enough—he was able to calculate that Earth was exactly 25,000 miles (40,225 km) around. This is almost precisely right!

ARISTARCHUS AND THE HELIOCENTRIC UNIVERSE

Perhaps the most remarkable work of any Greek philosopher was the model of the universe proposed by the great mathematician Aristarchus (310–250 B.C.). Aristarchus suggested that Earth was not at the center of the universe, as everyone had supposed until then. Instead, said Aristarchus, the sun was at the center of the universe, and Earth revolved around it. In fact, all of the planets revolved around the sun—except for the moon, which revolved around Earth. Why did the sun and planets *appear* to go around Earth? Because Earth was turning like a top, revolving once every day, and we were turning with it. Thus, an observer on the surface of Earth would see the heavens spin past on a daily schedule.

This was a revolutionary idea! It is remarkably close to the way we now know that the universe actually is. Of course, the sun isn't really at the center of the universe—in fact, there isn't any place that can properly be called the center of the universe—but the sun is at the center of the solar system, that is, the system of planets that includes Earth, the moon, other planets that the ancients knew about, and a few that they didn't know about.

Aristarchus's model of the universe is sometimes referred to as the *heliocentric universe*, from Greek words meaning "sun-centered." But in Aristarchus's time, most people believed that Earth was at the center of the universe, and the stars and planets revolved around it. This is called the *geocentric universe*, from Greek words meaning "Earth-centered."

Was Aristarchus hailed as one of the greatest of all scientists for proposing this heliocentric universe? No. In fact, the idea was largely ignored.

Why didn't the Greeks embrace the heliocentric universe? For several reasons. As we've noted already, it's quite obvious to any observer that the sun goes around Earth, not Earth around the sun. While an intelligent observer might agree that this may be an illusion caused by the spinning of Earth, there is certainly no reason to believe in such a thing without more compelling evidence. Besides, if Earth is moving, why is it that we move along with it? When a person jumps into the air, for instance, why doesn't Earth move away before he or she can fall back to the ground? Since a person who leaps straight up always comes back down in the same spot, it is obvious that Earth is not moving.

There was another clue that told the Greeks that Earth did not move. If Earth moved around the sun once every year, then we would be constantly changing positions in relation to the stars. Some stars would be closer to us at one time of the year, when we were on one side of the sun, and some stars would be closer at other times of the year, when we were on the other side of the sun. Therefore, some stars should be brighter in the winter, when they were closer, and dimmer in the summer, when they were farther away. Other stars would be brighter in the summer and dimmer in the winter.

Astronomers have long been aware that this does not happen. The stars have the same brightness all year round. Of course, if the stars were very, very far away, the difference in brightness might be too small to see. But the Greeks knew that, for this to be true, the distance to the stars would be so great that the human mind could not imagine it. And so they decided that Earth must indeed be standing still.

ARISTOTLE AND
THE GEOCENTRIC
UNIVERSE

To many historians, the greatest philosopher of Greek times was Aristotle (384–322 B.C.). And it was Aristotle who created the model of the universe that most Greeks believed in. In fact, the Aristotelian model of the universe (as it is sometimes called) remained the most famous and widely accepted model of the universe for nearly fifteen hundred years!

Aristotle believed in the geocentric universe—that is, he felt that Earth was at the center of the universe and all of the other planets revolved around it. But Aristotle's model of the universe went far beyond this. He proposed that Earth was surrounded by a series of crystalline spheres, and the planets were embedded in these spheres. The spheres were concentric—that is, they were nestled around each other, with Earth in the center. Because they were crystal, they were transparent, and we could see all the way to the outermost spheres. The second to last sphere, moving outward from Earth, contained the stars.

The outermost sphere, which Aristotle called the *primum mobile* (or "first mover"), rotated under its own power. Its movement was then "passed on" to the other spheres, which also rotated, but not necessarily at the same speed as the outermost sphere. This explained why the planets moved at different rates than the stars, for instance. In some ways, Aristotle's spheres resemble the gear boxes of modern automobiles, where rotating gears of different sizes pass their motions one to another to control the speed and power of the automobile's wheels. In fact, Aristotle's universe contained many purely transparent spheres without planets in them at all, existing purely for the purpose of changing the motions of other spheres.

The innermost sphere of Aristotle's universe contained the moon, and therefore the region where human beings lived was sometimes referred to as the "sublunar realm"—the land beneath the moon! The sublunar realm was made of different stuff than the heavens. Aristotle proposed that Earth and its immediate surroundings were made of four "elements"—Earth, air, fire, and water. Each of these elements had its natural place—Earth at the center of the universe, water on top of Earth, air on top of water, and fire on top of the rest. This explained why solid objects (Earth) and water tended to fall, while air and fire seemed to rise. They were simply seeking their natural places in the Aristotelian scheme of things.

The heavens, on the other hand, were made of a fifth element, which Aristotle called ether. The heavens were perfect, and so ether was a perfect substance. One piece of evidence for this was that everything beyond Earth appeared to be circular, and the Greeks believed that the circle was the perfect shape. The spheres that surrounded Earth were perfect circles, and all movement in the heavens was circular. It could not be otherwise, because then it would not have been perfect. And everything in the heavens was either perfectly transparent, like Aristotle's crystal spheres, or perfectly white and shining, like the sun and the stars.

And yet anyone gazing at the moon could see that not everything beyond the earthly realm was perfect. There are dark and unseemly markings on the moon's surface. The Greeks explained this by supposing that "exhalations" from the imperfect Earth had polluted the innermost sphere, where the moon resided. Fortunately, the lunar sphere prevented this pollution from traveling any farther.

And what of comets? They didn't move in perfect circles. This was irrelevant, according to Aristotle. He believed that the comets were merely fires in Earth's atmosphere, another proof that fire was the outermost of the earthly elements.

PTOLEMY'S UNIVERSE

About 350 years after Aristotle, an astronomer named Ptolemy, who was probably either Greek or Egyptian though little is known about him today, drew on the work of Aristotle and wrote a book that defined the model of the universe for more than a thousand years. The book came eventually to be called the *Almagest* (derived from Arabic words meaning "the greatest compilation"), and it described a universe very much like the one that Aristotle had proposed, with a few important changes.

Ptolemy, like most astronomers until only a few hundred years ago, was troubled by the way in which the planets moved through the sky. We have already said that they moved in patterns that were different from those of the fixed stars. Even worse, though, they were not consistent in their own motions. Usually they moved from west to east relative to the fixed stars behind them, but at times they would slow down and even move the other way. This was called *retrograde motion*, and it was very difficult to explain why it happened. It was almost as though the planets were not moving in perfect circles, which went against all logical thought!

Aristotle had attempted to explain this by the way his spheres passed their motion from one to the other, but Ptolemy was not satisfied with this explanation. Instead, Ptolemy suggested that the stars moved on *epicycles*.

What is an epicycle? It is a kind of wheel rotating on the outside of a wheel, the way that a large ferris wheel will have smaller wheels around the edge where the passengers sit. The epicycle for each planet would be fixed on the sphere assigned that planet, but the planet itself would be on the epicycle, not the sphere. Because the epicycle could rotate in the opposite direction from

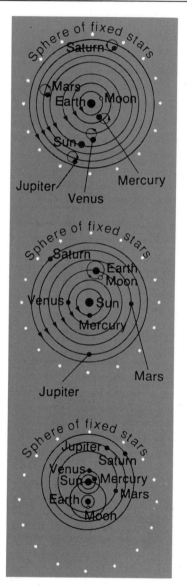

Aristotle believed in a geocentric universe, that is, Earth was the center of the universe, and the sun and the other planets revolved around it.

Copernicus believed in a heliocentric universe, with Earth and other planets orbiting the sun. However, he erred in believing that the orbits were perfect circles.

Tycho Brahe combined the theories of Aristotle and Copernicus, contending that the planets did revolve around the sun, but the sun revolved around Earth.

the big sphere, the planets would sometimes seem to move backward. Thus, Ptolemy explained retrograde motion.

Ptolemy's universe contained many of these epicycles, as well as a few more fancy mechanisms that we won't go into here. These epicycles seem rather ridiculous to us now, and in fact they may have seemed more than a little ridiculous then. But they were the best explanation that anyone could come up with for the way in which the planets appeared to move, and so they passed into the accepted lore of the astronomer for long centuries to follow.

And at that point progress in astronomy ceased. It was many centuries before anyone gave much thought to new models of the universe, new theories of the stars and planets. The Middle Ages had begun.

CHAPTER

THE COPERNICAN
REVOLUTION

The Middle Ages were a period of world history that lasted from about A.D. 400 to 1400, roughly a thousand years. It was not a good time for science. The thinking of philosophers in Europe was heavily influenced by the Christian Church. The Church, at least in the early Middle Ages, held that all knowledge must come from God and that the teachings of the Greek philosophers were contrary to the Bible. Hence, the ideas of Aristotle and Ptolemy were nearly forgotten in Europe.

Further to the east, however, the writings of the Greeks were kept alive by the Arabs, who translated the work of the Greek philosophers into their own language. If not for the Arabs, the teachings of the Greeks might have been lost forever, and modern civilization would be much the worse for it. Although much of what the Greeks believed about the universe was wrong, their thoughts and observations are nonetheless the foundation of much of what we know today, and their basic philosophy—that human beings could understand the universe through thought and reasoning—was an extremely important one.

In the late Middle Ages, the Europeans rediscovered the Greek philosophers. The great theologian/philosopher Thomas Aquinas (1225–1274) demonstrated that the model of the universe proposed by Aristotle was not contrary to the Bible. In fact, with a little work, it could be made to fit precisely with religious thought.

According to Aquinas, the "primum mobile" of Aristotle was actually God, and it was God that made the planets revolve in the heavens, through the assistance of angels. So appealing was this idea to the Church that it became the official Church doctrine, and any other notions about the universe were strongly discouraged.

And yet there were inevitably those who questioned the Aristotelian universe. One of the first of these was Nicolas Copernicus of Poland (1473–1543), who is remembered to this day as one of the greatest of all theoretical astronomers.

REDISCOVERING ARISTARCHUS

Copernicus rediscovered the theories of Aristarchus and was apparently quite taken with them. Aristarchus, you will recall, proposed that the sun was at the center of the universe, and that Earth and the other planets revolved around it. Copernicus liked this idea and decided it offered a better explanation of his own observations than did the Aristotelian model of the universe.

For one thing, it at least partially explained the phenomenon of retrograde motion. If Earth revolved around the sun with the other planets, then its own motion through space would occasionally overtake one of these planets and pass it by. Thus, it would seem to an observer on Earth as though the other planet had slowed down and moved backward, just as a moving automobile might seem to be moving backward to an observer in another automobile that was passing it.

To explain his ideas, Copernicus wrote a book called *De Revolutionibus Orbium Coelestium*, which is Latin for "On the Revolutions of the Celestial Spheres." (In Copernicus's time, most scholarly writings were in Latin.) It detailed his theories about the sun and planets.

Yet he hesitated to publish the book because he was afraid of negative reactions. What if he were ridiculed for his beliefs? Worse, what if the Church were to take offense at the suggestion that the now-approved Aristotelian universe was not correct? This was especially worrisome because Copernicus was an officer of the Church, albeit a minor one.

Fortunately for astronomy, Copernicus had several friends who believed that his theories were important, and they encouraged him to publish the book. Finally, though only after he had grown quite old, he agreed to have it published. He held the first printed copy of the book in his hands only a few hours before he died.

Despite Copernicus's fears, the book caused little excitement. In fact, most officials of the Church found it acceptable as an interesting hypothesis, though not as a real model of the way the universe worked. (One minor Church official actually managed to have a preface added to the book, unknown to Copernicus, in which it was suggested that the author did not really believe that Earth revolved around the sun but was merely saying so because it made his astronomical calculations easier!)

But Copernicus's ideas became more and more popular with time, and the Church became increasingly worried. In 1600, twenty-seven years after Copernicus's death, an Italian philosopher named Giordano Bruno was actually burned at the stake, at least in part because of his outspoken belief in the theories of Copernicus!

But the theories did not die, even if some of their supporters did. Slowly, the idea that Earth revolved around the sun began to catch on. Yet, surprisingly, one of the astronomers who did the most to popularize this idea was a man who didn't believe in it.

The Polish astronomer
Nicolas Copernicus

TYCHO'S
PARALLACTIC UNIVERSE

Tycho Brahe (1546–1601) was one of the most successful observational astronomers of all time. And he may have been the luckiest, lucky enough to catch the attention of the king of Denmark, who gave him his own private island and built an astronomical observatory for him.

Before that time, however, Tycho had already established himself in the world of astronomy through his observations of the nova of 1572. The word *nova*, which was coined by Tycho, means "new star." In 1572, Tycho (and millions of other people) saw a new star appear magically in the sky one night and remain there more than a year. Today, of course, we know that what Tycho saw was not a new star at all but a *supernova*, an old star that had exploded with incredible force. (We'll have more to say about supernovas in chapter nine.) Tycho made many observations of the nova and published a book about it, which made his reputation. The nova was a blow to those who believed, like Aristotle, that the heavens were perfect and unchanging.

Five years later, Tycho observed a comet, and disproved Aristotle's contention that comets were fires inside Earth's atmosphere. He did this with the aid of *parallax*.

What is parallax? It is an important concept in astronomy, and we will be coming back to it later, so it is important that you understand it. Parallax is the apparent change in relative position of objects when viewed from different positions.

How's that again? Let's look at an example. Suppose that you are standing in your front yard, looking at a pair of trees in a yard across the street, in such a position that one tree is directly behind the other. The second tree—the one behind the first tree—will be invisible, because it is hidden by the first tree. Now, suppose that you move slightly to one side. The second tree will seem to emerge from behind the first tree. As you move farther to one side, the two trees will seem to move farther and farther

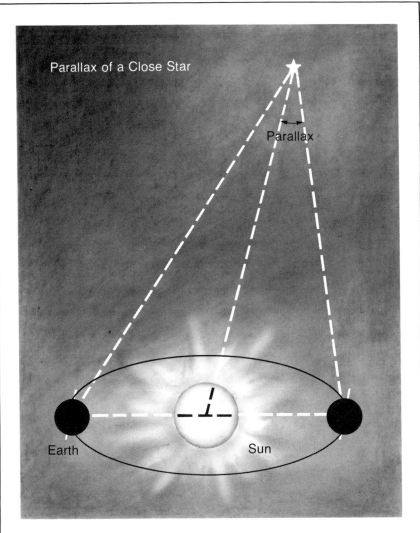

Parallax of a Close Star

Parallax

Earth

Sun

To measure a star's distance from Earth, the parallax of the star must first be determined.

apart, until they appear to be separated by a considerable distance when viewed against a distant background.

Yet the two trees haven't actually moved. You are just seeing them differently as you change positions. This change in apparent position of the two trees is called parallax. You can also see parallax among nearby objects simply by looking at them with one eye closed, and then with the other eye closed and the first eye open. In fact, this is how your brain produces three-dimensional vision using the data it receives from your two eyes, each of which sees your surroundings from a slightly different angle.

If a comet were a phenomenon in Earth's atmosphere, it should show parallax in relation to the stars behind it. That is, when viewed from two different positions on Earth's surface, it should seem to move against the background of stars.

Tycho showed that this was not the case. By measuring the position of the comet against the stars from several different positions on the ground, Tycho found no parallax at all. This meant that the comet must be very far away, since nearby objects show far more parallax than faraway ones. Therefore, the comets were outside Earth's atmosphere. This was another blow to those who believed in Aristotle's unchanging heavens.

With the financial help of the Danish king, Tycho built himself a collection of fine instruments for measuring the positions and movements of the stars and planets. He kept voluminous records of his observations, which were very important for the future of astronomy. His observations of the heavens were the most precise that anyone had made until that time.

It was clear from these observations that Aristotle was wrong. The universe was not a series of concentric spheres revolving around Earth. And yet, at the same time, Tycho could not bring himself to believe in Copernicus's notion that Earth revolved around the sun.

In a heroic effort, Tycho devised a theory that combined those of both Aristotle and Copernicus. Perhaps, said Tycho, the planets did revolve around the sun, as Copernicus had believed—but the sun revolved around Earth, as Aristotle had maintained! This bizarre synthesis managed to explain many of Tycho's observations while still remaining true enough to Aristotle to satisfy the Church.

JOHANNES KEPLER

But it did not satisfy everyone. Toward the end of his life, Tycho took a young astronomer under his wing. This astronomer was named Johannes Kepler (1571–1630). When Tycho died, he left all of his observations to Kepler and begged Kepler to use these observations to prove that his synthesis of the theories of Aristotle and Copernicus was true.

Kepler, however, had other ideas. He was convinced that Copernicus had been correct, and he set out to show exactly how the planets moved about the sun. And Tycho's observations were exactly what he needed to make his case.

Yet there were problems with Copernicus's theory, problems that troubled Kepler deeply. Although the Earth-centered universe helped to explain the phenomenon of retrograde motion, it didn't explain *everything* about the way the planets moved. In short, the motions of the planets were still unpredictable—and this worried Kepler very much.

Copernicus had worked his way around this problem by including epicycles in his theory, just as Ptolemy had. But Kepler did not like the epicycles and wanted to get rid of them. Yet there was no other way to explain the peculiar motions of planets.

Then one day the answer came to him, as though in a mystical vision. Copernicus, like all other astronomers since ancient times, had assumed that the planets moved in circles. But what if they didn't? Suppose, said Kepler, that the planets moved in *ellipses*.

What is an ellipse? It is a shape much like a circle—in fact, a circle is one kind of ellipse—but an ellipse can be more stretched out in one direction than a circle, rather in the way that a rectangle is a stretched-out square. If the planets, including Earth, were moving around the sun in ellipses instead of circles it would explain the peculiar motions that Tycho and other astronomers had observed.

Kepler had solved one of the great mysteries of the universe, but few astronomers were interested in listening. Kepler wrote a book about his theories and sent a copy to one of the greatest astronomers of all time. But the great astronomer, whom we will meet in the next chapter, apparently never read it. If he had, the history of astronomy might have taken a different course.

NEW EYES ON
THE SKY

What do you think of when you hear the word *astronomer*? Probably, you think of a person peering into an instrument called a *telescope*, looking at the sky. The telescope is such an important part of astronomy that it's hard to imagine what astronomy would be like without it.

And yet not one astronomer that we have talked about so far used a telescope, for the simple reason that the telescope was not yet invented. (Kepler used a telescope eventually, but only after he had developed the theories for which he is famous.) When these astronomers studied the sky, they used that most ancient of astronomical instruments: the naked eye.

We may laugh at the incorrect theories of Ptolemy and Tycho Brahe. Yet considering how limited their instruments were, compared to those available today, we can only be amazed that they learned as much as they did about the nature of objects in the skies. We can only imagine what Tycho Brahe would have learned with telescope in hand!

THE FIRST TELESCOPE

Nobody knows who invented the telescope. In fact, it may have been discovered quite by accident. One legend, which may or may not be fact, holds that an assistant of the Dutch lensmaker Hans Lippershey (1587–1619) was spending a lazy afternoon in the early 1600s playing with lenses when he accidentally discovered the secret of magnifying distant objects and making them seem nearby. It is even possible that Lippershey was sworn to silence about this discovery by the government, which recognized the potential of the telescope in warfare.

A telescope, in its simplest form, is a pair of lenses, one at each end of a long tube. The lenses are pieces of glass curved in such a way that they bend light and focus it onto a single point. By placing the right kind of lens at each end of the tube, the combined effect of the two lenses magnifies the image contained in the light, so that a person looking through one end of the telescope will see distant objects enlarged, as though they were closer than they actually are. Not only does it make distant objects seem larger, but it draws in more light from those objects than does the naked eye, so that dim objects become easier to see.

Despite any attempts to keep this instrument secret, word of its existence eventually spread to Italy, where it caught the attention of a scientist named Galileo Galilei (1564–1642).

Galileo was already an eminent figure in science by this time. He had made significant contributions to the science of physics, and he was very interested in astronomy. He was particularly interested in the theories of Copernicus, and when he saw a supernova in 1604, one that was also observed by Johannes Kepler, he took it as evidence that the heavens were not as perfect as Aristotle had thought they were. They could change in unexpected ways. And when he heard about the telescope, he immediately grasped its importance and built one of his own.

PEERING INTO SPACE

Galileo may have been the first astronomer to turn a telescope on the skies—and what he saw astounded him. The planet Jupiter had moons revolving around it, just as Earth did. The sun had dark spots on its surface, which marred its Aristotelian image of perfection. The planet Saturn had peculiar "handles" extending from it. (The great Dutch astronomer Christian Huygens [1629–1695] later realized that these were not handles but rings—the now-famous rings of Saturn—though Galileo did not know this during his lifetime.) And when he turned his telescope on the cloudy strip across the heavens that had long been known as the Milky Way, it turned out to be made of thousands and thousands of stars, too dim to be seen with the naked eye.

Galileo was convinced immediately that the theories of Copernicus were correct. Earth was not at the center of a universe made of perfect crystalline spheres. Rather, it was one of many planets that revolved around an imperfect sun, at least one of which was at the center of its own little system of revolving objects. And the universe was bigger than anyone had imagined, filled with countless stars that were doubtless full-blown suns in their own right, but so far away that even through the telescope they seemed to be no more than points of light.

THE STARRY MESSENGER

Unlike the shy and retiring Copernicus, Galileo was not hesitant to let the rest of the world know his thoughts about the universe, and in 1610 he published a book called *Siderius Nuncius* (The Starry Messenger). In this book, he described what he had seen through his telescope.

Naturally, the book created great excitement. Many people simply refused to believe that Galileo had seen the things he had, but others were sufficiently impressed to be converted to the theories of Copernicus.

Galileo was even able to demonstrate something that the Greeks could not: why a person leaping into the air is not left behind by the moving Earth. From his experiments as a physicist, Galileo knew that an object in motion tends to remain in motion unless something stops it. A person standing on Earth is in motion with Earth and retains that motion if he or she jumps into the air. Earth doesn't move out from beneath the person because he or she is moving right along with Earth.

Nonetheless, Galileo could not explain all of his observations of the heavens, at least not satisfactorily. For instance, Galileo still believed in the epicycles of Ptolemy because he had no better explanation for the motions of the planets. Kepler sent him copies of his book, but Galileo apparently never read them, and therefore he never grasped the idea that the planets moved in ellipses rather than perfect circles.

Also, like other astronomers of his time, Galileo was unable to answer the "why" of his observations. Why did the planets revolve around the sun? What force kept them from escaping into space? What made them move in circles, rather than in the straight lines that objects on Earth tended to move in?

Aristotle had believed that objects in the heavens moved according to different rules, or laws, than those on Earth. In the heavens, objects tended to move, and their motion was always circular. On Earth, objects tended to remain still, and when they moved they usually moved in a straight line. By Galileo's time, it was obvious (at least to Galileo) that objects in the heavens obeyed the same laws as those on Earth. Why, then, did heavenly objects move in great circles about the sun while objects on Earth remained generally still?

CHALLENGING THE CHURCH

Despite his inability to give satisfactory answers to these questions, Galileo's enthusiasm for the theories of Copernicus won many converts and brought him to the attention of the Church. Officials of the Church felt that Galileo's teachings were in direct contradiction to the Bible, which explicitly stated, or so they claimed, that Earth was motionless.

Galileo is brought before the Inquisition and forced
to renounce his claim that Earth moves.

Galileo was given a stern warning by the Church to stop preaching these theories, but he paid them little heed. Finally, at the age of seventy, he was brought before the Inquisition, a panel of Church officials that threatened him with severe punishment if he did not renounce his claim that Earth moved. Because he was old and sick, Galileo finally agreed to do so, although legend has it that he immediately muttered the words *"Eppur si muove!"* ("It still moves!") after his recantation.

But the Middle Ages were long over by then, and the power of the Church to tell people what to believe was weakening. The idea that Earth moves around the sun had now been planted in the minds of intelligent men and women throughout much of the world, and once planted the seed began to grow. It finally came to fruition in England, where the theories of Copernicus, Kepler, and Galileo were finally brought together by a man who was born in the year that Galileo died: Isaac Newton.

CHAPTER

A MATTER
OF GRAVITY

Isaac Newton (1642–1727) may be the greatest scientist who ever lived. He was a physicist, a theoretical astronomer, and a mathematician. He invented the form of mathematics known today as calculus, he devised the famous three laws of motion that govern everything from billiard balls to rocket ships to planets, and he described the force that holds the universe together and moves the planets as they circle the sun.

Not a bad piece of work for one lifetime!

THE APPLE THAT FELL
FROM THE TREE

What was the force that moved the planets and held the universe together? Newton looked at the astronomical theories of those who had come before him and saw the key element that they had all missed. And that key element was *gravity*.

Legend has it that Newton's inspiration came as he saw an apple fall from a tree to the ground and wondered if the apple was drawn to the earth by the same force that held the moon in its orbit. Unlike most such legends, this one is true.

Newton recognized that all matter in the universe produces a force called gravity. Gravity is an attractive force. That is, an

45—

object producing gravity—which is to say any object—attracts other objects toward it. The amount of gravity produced by an object depends on that object's mass. Mass is a property similar to weight. In fact, on the surface of Earth an object's mass and weight are the same. But in space, where an object has no weight, it still has mass. Objects without much mass, like rocks or human beings, don't produce much gravity. Massive objects— that is, objects with a lot of mass, like stars and planets—produce quite a lot.

The biggest object in the vicinity of Earth is the sun, and so it is the object that produces the most gravity. It is the sun's gravity that holds the planets in orbit around it. But Earth itself also produces gravity, and it is this gravity that holds the smaller moon in orbit around Earth. (It might occur to you that the moon also produces gravity, and you may wonder why Earth doesn't rotate about the moon instead. The truth is that Earth and its moon actually rotate about one another, with the center of their rotation being somewhere inside of Earth but not directly at the center. However, it is close enough to the center of Earth that it is fair to say that the moon goes around Earth rather than vice versa.)

LAWS OF MOTION

If the planets are attracted to the sun, though, why don't they simply fall into it? And why doesn't the moon fall to Earth just as Newton's apple did? The answer is that the moon and planets are in motion, and, as Galileo showed, an object in motion tends to remain in motion; Newton adopted this as one of his laws of motion. The gravity of the sun bends the orbits of the planets into an ellipse, but their motion prevents them from falling into it.

Newton demonstrated this principle with an analogy. Suppose you took a large cannon to the top of a mountain and fired a cannonball in a direction parallel to the ground below. The cannonball would fall to Earth, because it would be pulled downward by Earth's gravity, but it would not fall straight to Earth, because

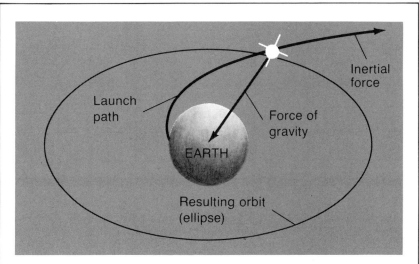

How an artificial satellite falls into orbit. As it proceeds on its launch path, the satellite is acted on by gravity and enters an elliptical orbit.

of its sideways motion. Rather, it would fall to Earth in a long curve, moving sideways and downward simultaneously. Since Earth is round, a cannonball with sufficient speed would actually fall right around the curve of Earth—and keep on falling forever! And this, in fact, is why the moon remains in orbit. It is like a giant cannonball, falling eternally around Earth. It is a *satellite* of Earth. In modern times, of course, we have been able to fire artificial satellites into orbit around Earth, using rockets rather than cannons. The principle, however, is exactly the same.

Newton gave us a profound understanding of the way our solar system works. The sun is a blazing ball of gas at the center, and the planets Mercury, Venus, Earth, Mars, Jupiter, and Saturn revolve around it, in immense ellipses called *orbits*. The moon, in turn, orbits Earth.

Finally, for the first time since human beings had turned their eyes on the stars, it seemed that the nature of the universe was completely understood.

Or was it? Well, no. Not really. There was a general feeling in Newton's time that all of the major questions about the universe had been answered, but that wasn't true. Only our small portion of the universe had been understood, and only incompletely. What Newton had done was to open a window, a window of understanding, through which astronomers could peer in their search for the secrets of the heavens. Now that Newton had shown the basic mechanism of our solar system, scientists were in a position to explore the nature of that mechanism and the universe of which it was part. A great age of discovery was only just beginning.

A BETTER TELESCOPE

Newton introduced one of the tools used in this new age of discovery: the *reflecting telescope*. The type of telescope used since the time of Galileo—the kind we have described as a tube with lenses at each end—is known as a *refracting telescope*. Unfortunately, there are certain limitations to the size of a refracting telescope that is practical to build, having to do with the length of the tube and the size of the lenses. Newton showed that it was possible to replace one of the lenses in the telescope with a curved mirror, hence the term "reflecting" telescope. This mirror, because it could be reinforced with a strong backing, could be made larger than the lenses in a refracting telescope, and thus reflecting telescopes could be built larger than refracting telescopes.

In Newton's time, the practical limit on the size of refracting telescopes had not yet been reached, but eventually the reflecting telescope all but replaced the refracting telescope for visual observation of the skies.

CHAPTER

THE REALM
OF THE
PLANETS

As it turned out, astronomers didn't even know everything there was to know about the planets in our solar system.

Since ancient times, it had been assumed that Saturn was the outermost planet. This meant that there were six planets in the solar system, counting Earth (which the ancients hadn't considered to be a planet) and not counting the sun and the moon (which the ancients did). The reason for this assumption, logically enough, was that these were (and still are) all of the planets that could be seen easily with the naked eye. And, until Galileo's time, the naked eye was all that anybody had to find planets with.

By Newton's time, however, it was obvious that there was more to the solar system than just these six planets.

There were, for instance, comets. These had been known since ancient times, but they had been assumed to be in Earth's atmosphere, not in the realm of the planets. Tycho, however, used parallax to prove that this was not true. But he was not able to explain precisely what comets were.

What made comets unusual among heavenly objects was their unpredictability. Unlike the planets, they came at odd moments and then disappeared, apparently never to return. In ancient times (and even in modern times, if the truth be told), this made comets a source of fear and consternation. Many people considered them omens of disaster because of this very unpredictability.

It was Isaac Newton who provided the key to the secret of comets, by showing how gravitation made the solar system go round. But it was Newton's friend Edmund Halley (1656–1742) who applied Newton's principles to comets in the most dramatic of all ways. And it was Halley whose name became inextricably connected with comets and remains so to this very day.

HALLEY'S COMET

At the age of twenty-four, Halley observed the comet of 1680. Two years later, in 1682, he observed another comet. By this time, his interest was definitely engaged. He made careful observations of the way comets behaved, and so he studied the comet of 1682 in great detail. He also investigated the history of comets, to find clues in the observations of astronomers of the past.

He discovered that several comets had behaved in a manner suspiciously similar to the comet of 1682, and that they had appeared in the years 1456, 1531, and 1607. Simple arithmetic informed Halley that these comets and the comet of 1682 had appeared at intervals of seventy-five or seventy-six years.

Could all of these comets be the same comet, returning every seventy-five and one-half years to the vicinity of Earth? Halley believed that they were.

What Halley determined was that the comet followed an elliptical orbit, just as the planets did. But in the case of the comet, the ellipse was extremely stretched out. In fact, one end of the orbit extended into the outer reaches of the solar system, way past the

Comet Halley as photographed when it reappeared in 1986, sporting a tail several million miles long

orbit of Saturn. But the other end of the orbit brought the comet very close to the sun. As the comet approached the sun, the sun's gravity pulled on it more strongly, which in turn increased the comet's speed. It raced through the Earth's skies in a few months, disappearing for several weeks into the glare of the sun, then reappearing for several more months on its way back into the outer solar system.

On its return trip, however, it was fighting against the sun's gravity, which caused it to slow down, until after more than three decades it fell back toward the sun and began the process over again. This is why the comet returned every seventy-five or seventy-six years.

Halley calculated the date of the comet's next appearance. Finally, he announced to the Royal Astronomical Society of England that the comet would return in 1758.

Halley did not live to see if he was correct; he would have been 102 years old when the comet made its next appearance. But on Christmas Day of 1758 the comet did indeed reappear, and it has been known as Halley's comet ever since. Its most recent appearance was in 1986, though it passed too far from Earth to present a very dramatic view.

DIRTY SNOWBALLS

What are comets made of? Halley didn't know, though they appeared to be some kind of gas or liquid because of their glowing, luminous tails. Many years later, the American astronomer Fred Whipple (b. 1906) suggested that they were "dirty snowballs," composed of ice and dust. When they approach the sun, a "wind" of tiny particles blowing out of the sun heats up the ice and causes a long stream of glowing particles to trail behind the comet, hence the comet's tail. Photographs of Halley's comet taken by space probes during its 1986 visit showed this to be true.

THE OORT CLOUD

Where did comets come from? This was another question that Halley wasn't prepared to answer. It was not until 1950 that the Dutch astronomer Jan Oort (b. 1900) theorized that comets came from a huge halo of ice chunks that surrounded the solar system at a distance of about two light years. (A light year is the distance that light travels in one year. It is about 6 trillion miles and is commonly used by astronomers as a measure of very large distances.)

According to Oort, this halo, or shell, is left over from the birth of our solar system. Occasionally, something happens to push one of the chunks of ice out of the sphere, and it falls toward the sun, becoming a comet. This halo of ice is known as the *Oort cloud*, in Oort's honor. We don't know if the Oort cloud actually exists, but it is the best guess we have today as to the origin of comets.

THE SEVENTH PLANET

So comets were part of the solar system after all! Like the planets, they circled the sun (although there are many comets that approach the sun only once and then return to the Oort cloud). Could there be more to the solar system than anyone up until Halley's time had suspected?

If there were, and it could be discovered with the aid of a telescope, it would certainly be found. In the years following Newton's and Halley's great work, stargazing became an increasingly popular hobby of educated men and women.

And yet, when the next truly major discovery about the solar system came, it was a complete surprise.

William Herschel (1738–1822) was a musician, an oboist who played in the Hanoverian Guards of Hanover, Germany. His real interests lay in astronomy, however, and he spent his evenings

studying the stars. He was also a lens grinder, and with the help of his sister Caroline (1750–1848), herself an accomplished astronomer, he built telescopes for his own use.

One night, while studying the heavens through one of these telescopes, he saw something that was most definitely not a star. It was too bright, almost a disk. No star, no matter how bright, appears as a disk through a telescope, even through the powerful telescopes available today. Herschel knew that he had discovered something new.

Just how new, he didn't know. At first, Herschel assumed that he was looking at a comet. But when he calculated its orbit, it was almost circular, like that of a planet. To his astonishment, Herschel realized that it *was* a planet, one that no one had known existed.

Herschel named the new planet Uranus, after a figure in Greek mythology. As it turned out, Herschel was not the first person, even the first astronomer, to see Uranus. In fact, it can just barely be seen with the naked eye. But he was the first to realize what he had seen. Uranus was the seventh planet of the solar system, orbiting the sun far beyond Saturn.

The public's imagination was greatly excited by Herschel's discovery. The very idea that there might be additional planets in the solar system was a new one. But now that this idea was abroad, it seemed natural to assume that there might be other planets beyond Uranus.

There was reason to believe that this might be true. Careful study of the orbit of Uranus showed that it behaved in a slightly

William Herschel is shown here studying the night sky. With him is his sister Caroline, also an accomplished astronomer.

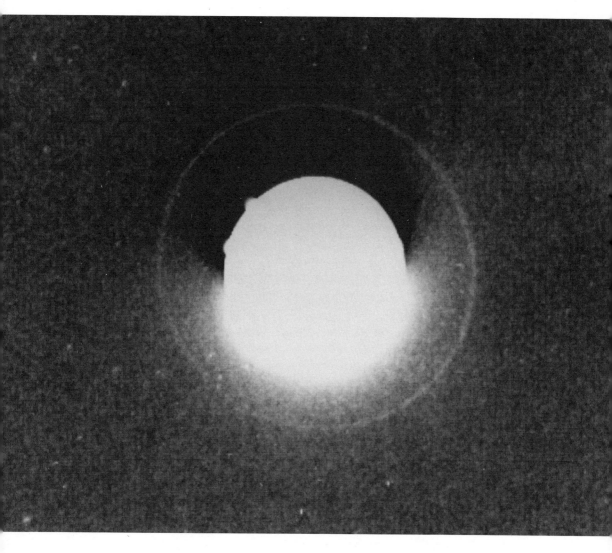

This composite photograph of Uranus was taken by the Voyager 2 spacecraft and shows the planet's outermost ring, one of nine rings now known to exist.

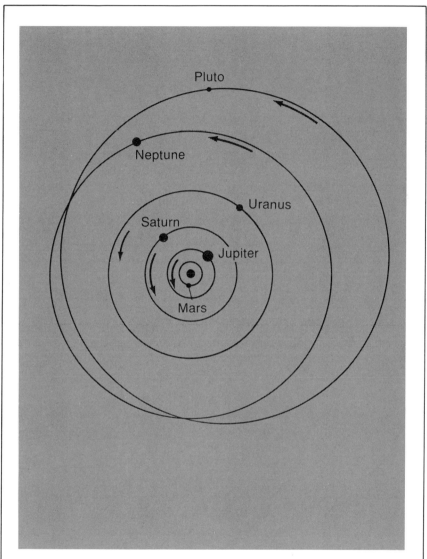

The direction in which the outer planets revolve around the sun

odd manner that might be explained if it were being affected by the gravity of a planet even farther away from the sun. The position of this undiscovered eighth planet was predicted on the basis of Uranus's orbit, and astronomers began to search for it in earnest.

A PLANET
NAMED NEPTUNE

The credit for discovering the eighth planet goes to three different men in three different countries. The first to see the planet was the German astronomer Johann Galle (1812–1910). But he had been told where to look by the French astronomer Urbain Jean Joseph Leverrier (1811–77), who had calculated the planet's position with uncanny precision. As it turned out, however, the planet's position had been predicted a year earlier by the English astronomer John Couch Adams (1819–1892), but no one had gotten around to looking for it. Hence, Adams, Leverrier, and Galle all share credit for the discovery, though the lion's share of the credit is usually reserved for Adams and Leverrier, who did the truly difficult part of the work. Galle simply looked at the right spot in the sky.

PLANET X

Was Neptune the last planet in the solar system? You may know the answer to that question already. No, it was not. Excited by the discovery of Neptune, astronomers began the search for an even more distant planet from the sun, by studying peculiarities in the orbits of other planets that might be caused by the gravity of still unknown planets.

One astronomer who spent much of his career looking for this ninth planet was Percival Lowell (1855–1916), who is better remembered today for his claim that the surface of the planet Mars was crisscrossed by "canals." (We now know that the canals do not exist, but Lowell honestly believed that they had been built by a dying Martian civilization.) Lowell called the ninth planet "Planet X," but he never found it.

Planet X was finally discovered in 1930, by the American astronomer Clyde Tombaugh (b. 1906). Using the facilities of the Lowell Observatory (named after the same Lowell who had fruitlessly searched for the planet), Tombaugh discovered the ninth planet by spending a full year comparing photographs of the sky taken at different times, to see if any starlike objects moved between photographs, as a planet would. When he finally located the planet, he called it Pluto, after the Roman god of the underworld. He chose the name because it began with the letters *P* and *L*, which were Percival Lowell's initials.

Pluto is a peculiar planet. Its orbit is much more elliptical than those of the other planets. A portion of its orbit actually swings inside the orbit of Neptune for about twenty years of its 248-year orbit around the sun. In fact, until about the year 2000, Pluto will be the eighth planet outward from the sun and Neptune the ninth!

THE "TENTH" PLANET

Is Pluto the last planet to be discovered in our solar system? So far it is. Some astronomers have suggested that there might be a tenth planet, beyond the orbits of Pluto and Neptune, but no one has identified it yet.

There may almost have been a tenth planet between the orbits of Mars and Jupiter. In the eighteenth century two scientists, Johann Titius (1729–96) and Johann Bode (1747–1826), separately suggested that there was a mathematical relationship in the distances between the planets, moving outward from the sun. However, there was a hole in this relationship, between Mars and Jupiter. There should be a planet there, Bode suggested.

When Herschel discovered Uranus and astronomers began

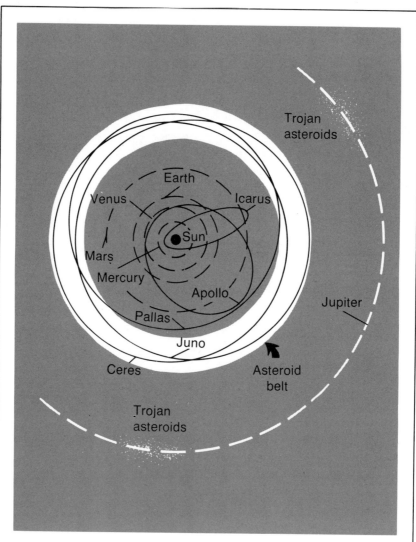

Most asteroids are located in the asteroid belt between Mars and Jupiter.

searching earnestly for new planets, one of the places that they looked was between the orbits of Mars and Jupiter.

Instead of a planet they found *planetesimals*—tiny planets—and lots of them. Today we know these small rocky bodies as *asteroids*. There are many thousands of them, too small to qualify as full-fledged planets, most of them orbiting the sun between Mars and Jupiter. The first was discovered in 1801 and was named Ceres, though at first it was thought to be a star.

It has been theorized that the asteroids may be the remains of a planet that once existed but somehow fell apart. More likely, though, they are the pieces of a planet that never formed—almost, but not quite, the tenth planet of the solar system.

The solar system can be considered Earth's immediate neighborhood in space, and it is the part of the universe that was the main concern of astronomers from ancient times until the early twentieth century.

But even the ancients were aware that something lay beyond the outermost planets: the realm of the stars. And although Aristotle probably never suspected it, this realm was much larger than any ancient astronomer dared to guess.

7

THE REALM
OF THE STARS

How big is the universe? This is a tough question, and it may not even have a meaning. It implies that the universe has a size, and to have a size something must have limits. Does the universe have limits? Or does it go on forever? These, you may recall, were some of the tricky questions that our young villager grappled with in the first chapter, and they have been questions that astronomers have grappled with ever since.

Aristotle thought that the universe ended in the primum mobile, which lay beyond the sphere of the fixed stars. And how far away was the primum mobile? That was impossible to say, since it was invisible. You'll recall, however, that the Greeks refused to believe in Aristarchus's moving Earth because it would have made the stars look different at different times of the year unless the stars were very, very far away. This meant that the Greeks must have thought the stars were relatively nearby, probably at a distance measurable in millions of miles. (This may seem like quite a distance, but compared to the actual distance of the stars it is barely a hop, skip, and a jump.)

THE INFINITE UNIVERSE

But when Galileo turned his telescope on the sky and saw vast numbers of hitherto unsuspected stars, too dim to be seen with the naked eye, it became obvious that the universe was larger than anybody had suspected. It was filled with uncountable stars, each of which was a sun in its own right and might well be surrounded by planets, as our sun was. In fact, the suspicion began to grow that the universe might not have an end, that the stars might go on forever, for an infinite distance into space.

In 1826 the German astronomer Heinrich Wilhelm Olbers (1758–1840) pointed out that this could not be the case. If the universe were infinite and filled evenly with stars, then everywhere we looked in the sky we would see a star. The night sky could not be dark. It would be filled with a bright white glow! And yet the night sky is dark. This apparent contradiction is called *Olbers' Paradox,* and it is pretty convincing proof that the universe is not infinitely large.

In gauging the size of the universe, it would help if we could at least measure the distance to the stars. But how can we measure the distance to something we cannot touch?

One way might be to measure how bright the star appears to be. You've probably noticed that a bright object, such as a candle or a light bulb, looks brighter when you are close to it than when you are far away from it. The same is true of stars. By measuring the brightness of a star, we might be able to tell how far away it is. The problem with this method is that we first must know how bright the star is to begin with—that is, how bright it would be if we saw it up close. And this isn't always possible.

In the seventeenth century, Christian Huygens attempted to measure the distance to the star Sirius using this method. He assumed that Sirius was probably about as bright as our sun, then calculated how far away it must be to appear as bright as it actually does. He calculated that Sirius must be 2.5 trillion miles away.

Unfortunately, Huygens made a poor choice of stars. Sirius is actually many times brighter than our sun, and so his calculations fell quite short of the actual distance, which we now know to be about 50 trillion miles!

The secret of measuring the distance to stars—at least, the distance to nearby stars—turned out to be parallax, the same method Tycho used to demonstrate that comets were not in Earth's atmosphere.

Parallax, you'll remember, is the way that an object seems to change position relative to other objects when looked at from different angles. On Earth, surveyors use the parallax to measure distances through a process called triangulation. By looking at an object from two different positions and measuring the apparent change in position of that object against a distant background, the surveyor can calculate the distance to the object using a kind of mathematics called trigonometry.

If astronomers could find a star that displayed parallax—that is, a star that seemed to move against the background of stars when seen from two different positions—they could measure the distance to the star. This wasn't easy to do. Since ancient times, astronomers had looked for this so-called stellar parallax and had never seen it.

But the invention of the telescope improved the ability of astronomers to measure changes in the position of a star. Finally, in 1838, the German astronomer Friedrich Wilhelm Bessel (1784–1846) spotted a small parallax in the star called 61 Cygni. To find the parallax, it was necessary to view the star from two places very far away from one another—the two sides of Earth's orbit. Bessell measured the star at intervals six months apart, when Earth (and therefore Bessel himself) was on opposite sides of the sun. This meant that his observations were separated by nearly 200 million miles—and still there was barely any change in the star's position against the backdrop of more distant stars.

Based on its parallax, Bessel calculated that 61 Cygni was eleven light years away, or 66 trillion miles. Shortly after Bessel made this discovery, the Scottish astronomer Thomas Henderson (1798–1844) showed that the star Alpha Centauri, which also showed a small parallax, was only 4.33 light years from Earth. (The closest star to Earth known today, aside from our own sun, is Proxima Centauri, which circles around Alpha Centauri and comes slightly closer to us at times than Alpha Centauri does.)

From these measurements, it was clear that the stars were indeed very far away, which explained why the Greeks saw no difference in the appearance of the stars from one half of Earth's orbit to the other. And these were only the nearest of stars! Most stars are much farther away from us.

It would seem, then, that the stars did stretch on forever, or something very near to it. And yet Olbers had shown that this could not be true. How could astronomers resolve this paradox?

THE MILKY WAY

One clue has been visible since ancient times. It is the luminous strip of light called the Milky Way, which stretches all the way across the sky, from one horizon to the other. When Galileo turned his telescope on the Milky Way, it turned out to be made up of many millions of distant stars. Yet when he turned his telescope in other directions, comparatively few distant stars were visible.

Thus, most of the distant stars were concentrated in a relatively narrow portion of the sky. It was as though the stars had taken the formation of a giant circle, or disk. The Greek word for the Milky Way was *galaxias* (which means roughly the same thing as Milky Way), and so this giant disk of stars came to be called the *galaxy.*

Because the Milky Way is spread evenly all around us, most astronomers assumed that we were located directly in the middle of the galaxy. In the 1920s, however, the American astronomer Harlow Shapley (1885–1972) determined that we were actually near the edge of the galaxy, but were unable to see all the way to the center (which would have been obviously brighter in the sky than the rest of the Milky Way) because it was hidden by dark clouds of dust.

If all of the stars were concentrated into the disk of the galaxy, did this mean that the universe actually had a shape, and an edge? What lay beyond that edge? Nothing? Empty space? Is the galaxy all there is to the universe?

THE SEARCH FOR OTHER GALAXIES

This was the subject of a great debate between astronomers that lasted well into this century. The main subjects of this debate were fuzzy objects called *nebulae* (plural of *nebula*), most of which are not visible to the naked eye but which are plentiful when viewed through a telescope.

In the eighteenth century, the French astronomer Charles Messier (1730–1817) compiled a catalog of many of these objects. Messier was a comet hunter, and he compiled his catalog chiefly to warn his fellow comet hunters that these objects were not comets. As it turned out, Messier is much better remembered today for his catalog of these objects than for any comets that he discovered. In fact, many nebulae are still referred to by names like M31 and M33, which indicate their positions in the Messier catalog.

For many years astronomers assumed that the nebulae were clouds of gas or dust, for the simple reason that they had the fuzzy look of gas clouds, like the tails of comets. But a few astronomers dared to suggest that, like the Milky Way, they may be great clouds of stars, so far away that the individual stars could not be seen, even through telescopes.

However, by the twentieth century, astronomers had a powerful new tool at their disposal: the photographic plate. As we saw earlier, one of the advantages of the telescope is that it draws in more light than does the human eye, and therefore receives more detail in the images of distant objects.

By using an instrument that is part camera and part telescope, astronomers could make a time exposure—that is, they could leave the photographic paper in the telescope for hours at a time, so that it could absorb tremendous amounts of light from space. When the photograph was examined later, the astronomer could see details that could not be seen by putting the naked eye to the telescope's eyepiece.

By taking photographs of the nebulae it was finally possible to make out, very dimly, individual stars within the bright clouds of a few of them. The nebulae turned out to be clouds of stars! (Actually, some nebulae also turned out to be clouds of dust and gas after all.)

Were these clouds of stars distant galaxies in their own right, like our Milky Way galaxy? Or were they smaller clusters of stars in or just outside our galaxy? (Such clusters of stars actually exist. They are called *globular clusters*, and they lie in a giant sphere around the center of the Milky Way. In fact, Shapley used these clusters to locate the center of our galaxy.)

MEASURING SPACE

To find out, we would need to measure the distance to these galaxies. A way to do just this was discovered in 1904 by the American astronomer Henrietta Swan Leavitt (1868–1921). She was studying a type of star known as the *Cepheid variable*. These stars change brightness over a period of time, becoming dimmer, then brighter, then dimmer again. Although different Cepheid stars take a different amount of time to go through this cycle, any particular Cepheid always takes the same amount of time to go from bright to dim and back again.

Leavitt noticed that there was a direct relationship between the brightness of a Cepheid variable and the amount of time it took to go through its cycle. This meant that an astronomer could tell how bright a Cepheid was by timing its cycle, even if it was very far away.

Earlier, we saw that brightness could be used as a way of measuring the distance to a star if we knew how bright the star

Henrietta Swan Leavitt discovered a way
to measure distances in space.

was to begin with. Although this isn't possible with most stars—a dim star, for instance, might be a star that is very dim and close to us or very bright and very far away—it is quite possible with Cepheids, because we can tell how bright they are by measuring their cycles.

OUR NEIGHBOR, ANDROMEDA

In the 1920s, the American astronomer Edwin Hubble (1889–1953) began searching for Cepheid variables in photographs of the M31 galaxy, sometimes called the Great Nebula in Andromeda. (This is the only other galaxy visible with the naked eye from the Northern Hemisphere, although it can be seen only on a very clear night in a very dark place.)

Hubble found his Cepheids and used them to determine the distance to the galaxy. Although his initial estimates were somewhat short, it eventually turned out to be 2 million light years away, which means that light from the Andromeda galaxy takes 2 million years to reach our eyes! It was also much larger than our own galaxy, proving once and for all that there are full-fledged galaxies beyond our own. In fact, there turned out to be billions of them.

THE EXPANDING UNIVERSE

Hubble proceeded to measure the distances to many other galaxies, and he made an astonishing discovery. When he looked at the light from galaxies beyond the immediate vicinity of our own, he discovered a peculiar thing. The light had become red-shifted. A *red shift* is a change in the wavelength of the light. (We'll have more to say about wavelengths in the next chapter.) The red shift means that the galaxies are moving away from us, causing the waves of light from the galaxy to become "stretched out."

In fact, every galaxy not in our immediate vicinity is red-shifted. Furthermore, the farther away a galaxy is, the more red-shifted it is—that is, the more stretched out its light waves are, and, therefore, the faster it is racing away from us. It's as if the entire universe, except for the local group of galaxies of which the Milky Way and Andromeda galaxy are part, is fleeing from us! We seem to be in the midst (though not necessarily the middle) of an *expanding universe*!

Why should the universe be expanding? Why should all of the galaxies be racing apart? Astronomers could only guess that at one time all of the matter in the universe had been compressed into a tiny point. Then there had been a huge explosion, in which all of that matter had been flung outward to form the universe. The Russian-American physicist George Gamow (1904–1968) dubbed this explosion the *Big Bang.* It probably took place about 20 billion years ago.

DISTANT QUASARS

Because distant galaxies are more red-shifted than the nearer ones, astronomers could use the red shift of a galaxy to determine its distance. The red shift became a method of measuring the distance to the most distant objects in the universe.

And how far have astronomers been able to see across this expanding universe? The most distant objects seen to date are the *quasars*, short for "quasi-stellar objects." When the quasars were first photographed, astronomers thought that they were dim stars in our own galaxy. Then they noticed that the quasars had the largest red shifts of any objects yet photographed.

*Edwin Hubble measured
the distances to many
other galaxies.*

Therefore, they must be farther away than any objects previously seen. To produce enough light to be seen over such distances, they must be at least a hundred times brighter than entire galaxies. Yet there is reliable evidence that the quasars are no larger than, say, our solar system. How could an object so small produce enough energy to appear so bright?

No one knows for sure, but some astonishing answers have been proposed. Before we can look at those answers, though, we'll have to take a detour into the bizarre world of twentieth-century physics, where matter is made of energy and space itself can become curved.

The Andromeda galaxy

CHAPTER

THE REALM
OF THE
INCREDIBLE

What is physics? It is the science that studies the relationship between matter and energy, between the things that the universe is made of and the forces that hold them together.

Physics and astronomy have always gone hand in hand. Newton was a physicist as well as a theoretical astronomer. Galileo was a physicist before he became an observational astronomer. Physics helps the astronomer to understand how the stars and planets work. Astronomy shows us the laws of physics in action.

In the first part of the twentieth century, the science of physics went through a major upheaval. Much of what scientists believed to be true turned out to be only partly true, and the complete truth turned out to be quite incredible. In this chapter, we'll tell you about a few things that physicists have learned in this century, then show you what this has meant to astronomers. In some cases, it has led to discoveries in astronomy that are nothing short of astonishing.

THE NATURE OF LIGHT

In Sir Isaac Newton's time, it was believed that light was a kind of wave, like waves in water or sound waves in air. By using a prism to break rays of white light into their component parts, Newton showed that white light is made up of light of many different wavelengths and that each wavelength is a different color. (The length of a wave—or wavelength—is the distance between two neighboring high points of a wave.) The rainbow assortment of colors produced when light is broken up into its various wavelengths is called a *spectrum.* You have seen a spectrum if you (like Newton) have ever played with a prism—or, for that matter, if you have seen a rainbow.

Today we know that light isn't exactly a wave in the sense that sound is a wave or that waves in water are waves, but it does have many of the characteristics of a wave, including a wavelength. We also know that what we call visible light is actually part of a much larger spectrum, called the *electromagnetic spectrum,* which also includes infrared light, ultraviolet light, gamma rays, x rays, and radio waves (which include television waves). These are all forms of *electromagnetic radiation.* The only difference between visible light and these other forms of electromagnetic radiation is in wavelength. Some of these waves have long wavelengths, some have short wavelengths, some have medium-size wavelengths—but they are all electromagnetic waves.

Why is this important to astronomy? Because for thousands of years astronomers had one means of studying the stars— visible light. This light carries valuable information, and astronomers have learned much from it. And yet stars are also producing other sorts of electromagnetic radiation, and this radiation also carries information.

In 1931, an engineer for the Bell Telephone Laboratories named Karl Guthe Jansky (1905–1950) accidentally discovered that strange radio waves were emanating from the sky—and that most of them were coming straight from the center of our galaxy! The only explanation for these radio waves was that they were produced by stars and other objects in the sky. Because the largest nearby concentration of these objects is in the center of our galaxy, that is where Jansky's radio waves were strongest.

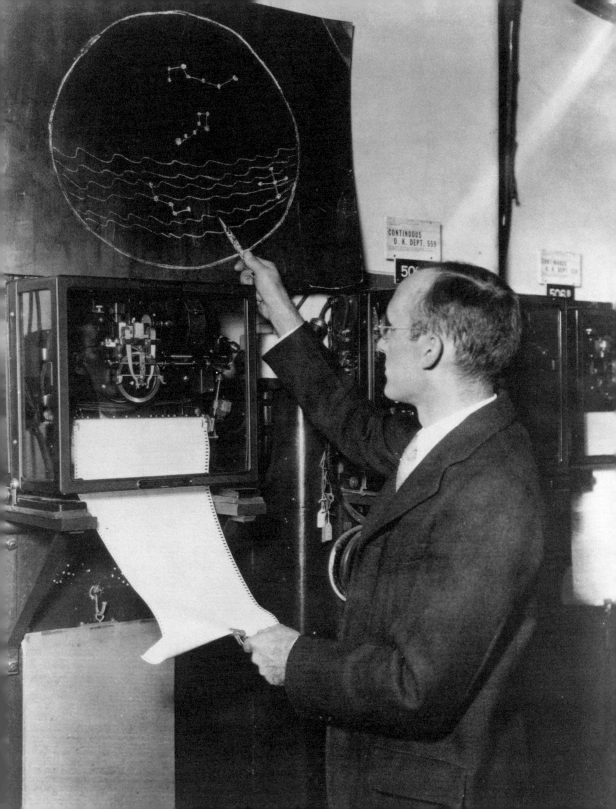

Thus was born the science of *radio astronomy*, in which astronomers use giant radio antennas, called *radio telescopes*, to detect radio waves from space. One of the important advantages of radio astronomy, as demonstrated by Jansky's discovery, is that it can detect radio waves from places from which visible light cannot reach us, such as the center of the galaxy.

If it is possible to build radio telescopes, is it also possible to build x-ray telescopes, and gamma-ray telescopes, and infrared telescopes, and ultraviolet telescopes? Yes, it is. Unfortunately, these forms of electromagnetic radiation cannot pass through Earth's atmosphere. (Actually, this is quite fortunate for human beings in general, because we would be killed by some of these radiations if they *could* pass through the atmosphere, but it makes life difficult for astronomers who would like to study the sky at these wavelengths.)

The solution was to put such telescopes in artificial satellites, so that they could orbit high above Earth's atmosphere, where they are free to observe just about any kind of electromagnetic radiation coming out of the heavens. These new telescopes have revolutionized astronomy, giving astronomers vast amounts of data about the universe that they were unable to receive through visible light.

THE NATURE OF MATTER AND ENERGY

In 1905, the physicist Albert Einstein (1879–1955) published his special theory of relativity. Einstein, who is generally regarded as

Karl Jansky is shown pointing to the position on a chart where radio noises from space were first heard.

the greatest scientist since Isaac Newton, proposed ideas in this paper that still sound bizarre today, more than eighty years after it was published. But all of these ideas have become an accepted part of modern physics and therefore of astronomy. One of them is that matter and energy are interchangeable—that is, solid matter can be turned into pure energy and vice versa. This theory eventually led to the development of the atomic and hydrogen bombs, which turn a tiny bit of matter into a lot of energy, in the form of a devastating explosion.

Einstein's theory answered a question that astronomers had been asking for many years: What makes the stars burn? The answer is *hydrogen fusion.*

Physicists have known since the early nineteenth century that all matter is made up of extremely tiny particles called atoms. Different kinds of matter—that is, different elements, such as oxygen, hydrogen, helium, lead, iron, and so forth—are made up of different kinds of atoms. Twentieth-century physicists learned that these atoms are, in turn, made up of even smaller subatomic particles, called electrons, protons, and neutrons.

Under very high temperatures, atoms can be broken apart and put back together, or fused, to form new types of atoms. This process is called fusion and usually involves hydrogen atoms that are broken apart and put back together to form helium atoms. During this process (which we have simplified considerably here), a tiny bit of matter from the atoms changes into pure energy.

A star is born when a cloud of gas and dust floating in space collapses under its own gravity. Friction between the atoms in the

Albert Einstein delivering a lecture to the American Association for the Advancement of Science in December of 1934

cloud produces heat, and this heat eventually causes fusion to take place. As huge numbers of atoms fuse together, huge amounts of energy are released—and this produces the light and heat of the star.

But what happens to a star that runs out of hydrogen atoms to fuse into helium atoms? Well, if it is a fairly small star, it will simply burn out and collapse under its own weight. It will become very small, and very dense and heavy. It will remain hot and glowing for many billions of years, like a burning cinder left over from a fire. Such a star is called a *white dwarf.*

The first white dwarf was discovered in 1844 by Friedrich Wilhelm Bessel, although he did not realize what he had found. He noticed that the star Sirius had a peculiar wobble to it, which seemed to indicate the presence of a large object in its vicinity producing a lot of gravity. Bessel knew that many stars were part of multiple star systems—that is, solar systems with more than one star in them. He assumed that Sirius must have at least one companion star, and yet he could not see such a star through his telescope. Finally, in 1862, astronomer Alvan Clark (1832–1897) spotted the companion star through his telescope—and it was very small. How could it be producing enough gravity to make Sirius wobble? The answer is that, although small, the star was also very massive, containing within it almost all of the matter of a normal star squeezed into a very small space. It was a white dwarf.

What happens when a larger star runs out of hydrogen and dies? The answer is that it also collapses—but then it explodes. The gravity of the larger star causes new types of fusion to take place, involving elements other than hydrogen. These fusion reactions produce huge amounts of heat, and the star balloons up to many times its original size, becoming a red giant, a huge and bloated star. But the red giant eventually burns up all of its fuel as well, and collapses again. This time the collapse generates so much heat that the outer layers of the star are blown off in a tremendous explosion. This explosion is a supernova, just like the ones Tycho, Kepler, and Galileo observed. (Ironically, there have been no supernovas visible in this galaxy since the invention of the telescope, although astronomers have been able to study supernovas in other galaxies.) As it explodes, the star briefly produces as much energy as many billions of stars.

What remains of the star after the explosion then collapses, much like a white dwarf, but the extra gravity of the large star causes a more violent collapse. The atoms that make up the star disintegrate under the pressure. The star becomes a superdense, superhot ball of neutrons. We call such a star a *neutron star.*

In 1967, the astronomer Jocelyn Bell detected strange bursts of radio waves from space on the radio telescope at the Cambridge University Observatory. These radio signals were so regular and even that astronomers were briefly tempted to suspect they were signals from an intelligent race of beings in outer space. The source of the signals was dubbed a *pulsating star*, or *pulsar* for short.

More pulsars were soon discovered. The source of one pulsar signal turned out to be the Crab Nebula, a cloud of gas in space believed to be the remains of a supernova observed by Chinese astronomers in 1054. Could the source of the signals be a neutron star left over from the explosion? Almost certainly it was. Apparently the neutron star is spinning at high speeds, creating strange electromagnetic vibrations that shoot out into space as radio waves.

Finally, what happens to an *extremely* large star that runs out of hydrogen? The answer, once again, is that it collapses, turns into a red giant, then explodes as a supernova, just like the stars that become neutron stars. But then it collapses again—and something happens that is strange indeed!

THE NATURE
OF GRAVITY

In 1915, Einstein published yet another paper, called the general theory of relativity. In it, he attempted to answer a question that had eluded even Newton: What is gravity? Why should objects produce a force that attracts other objects?

Einstein's answer was that gravity was not a force at all, in the sense that it was something that reached out over a distance and acted on another object. Rather, gravity was a curve in space.

A curve in space? How can space be curved?

This is not an easy question to answer, because it involves thinking of space in a brand-new fashion, as though it were *something* rather than *nothing.* Although it is traditional to think of space as being the absence of everything, Einstein thought of space as being as every bit as real as matter. According to Einstein, space could be bent by the presence of an object, just as the top of a metal table might be bent if you dropped a heavy bowling ball on it.

Having more mass than most objects, stars "bend" space more severely than, say, bowling balls. Objects such as planets in the vicinity of a star have their motion affected by this bend in space. This is why the normal straight-line motion of the planets in the solar system is bent into elliptical motion by the gravity of the sun. They are actually moving around the edge of an elliptical "hole" in space created by the presence of the sun's mass. Similarly, we can't simply jump off the surface of Earth, because we are at the bottom of a hole created by Earth's mass. Only a powerful rocket moves fast enough to climb out of this hole and into outer space.

In an extremely powerful gravitational field, weird things can happen. And this takes us back to the collapse of the extremely large star. After its fuel is exhausted, the star will collapse with such force that even the neutrons will be crushed. Space around the star will be bent so severely that the star will vanish from the normal universe. Even the light produced by the star will be unable to escape. It will become a *black hole.*

Strange things will happen in the vicinity of the black hole. According to Einstein's theory, the intense gravity of the hole will cause time to slow down. At the center of the black hole, the very laws of physics may break down and cease to operate. Physicists are unable to tell us what would take place within the black hole.

Have we ever seen a black hole? How could we? A black hole would be invisible!

Still, it would produce evidence that it was there. Any other objects near the black hole would be sucked into it by its gravity. The hole would probably be surrounded by a cloud of gas and dust slowly spiraling into it. Friction would make this cloud, called an *accretion disk*, very hot, perhaps hotter than just about anything else in the universe. It would produce intense bursts of x rays, one of the most energetic kinds of electromagnetic radiation. Such x rays have been detected, by x ray telescope, coming from the constellation Cygnus. There may be a black hole there, although astronomers are not yet sure.

We may even be seeing black holes in other galaxies. What would happen if a black hole occurred in the center of a galaxy? Well, stars are much thicker in a galactic center than they are in the fringes, so it is possible that the black hole would begin "eating" other stars around it, sucking them in with its intense gravity. As it ate other stars, it would become larger, perhaps swallowing thousands and thousands of other stars. The cloud of matter surrounding such a black hole would be so hot and huge that it could be seen for billions of miles!

Could this be what quasars are? Many astronomers think so. Why do we see only quasars billions of miles away? Why are there no quasars nearby? Remember that the light from distant galaxies takes a long time to reach us, so that we are really seeing these galaxies as they were in the long-ago past. When we see a quasar, we are looking back billions of years, much of the way back to the Big Bang itself! Perhaps quasars are an event that takes place early in the life of galaxies. By the time galaxies grow older, like the galaxies in the vicinity of our own, these black hole explosions have calmed down, though they have probably not gone away. And, in fact, there is evidence that there are explosions taking place in nearby galaxies, though they are not as violent as the quasar explosions. Exploding galaxies are called Seyfert galaxies, after the astronomer who first identified them, and they may contain giant black holes at their centers.

There has even been evidence uncovered recently that our own galaxy has just such a black hole explosion taking place at its center. We cannot see the center of our galaxy with visible light, but we can detect other forms of radiation from the center, and they indicate that something violent is going on. Perhaps our galaxy was once a quasar, many billions of years ago. And perhaps it now has a black hole in its center, swallowing stars by the thousands!

Einstein's theory of gravitation may also provide the answer to another question that has troubled stargazers since at least the time of the innocent villager in the first chapter. Does the universe go on forever? Or does it have an end? And if it has an end, what lies beyond it?

Einstein tells us that the universe can be infinite and yet not have an edge. The gravity of all of the galaxies in the universe may bend space into a great sphere, so that the universe curves in on itself. A space traveler who traveled outward into space, away from Earth, would eventually return to where he or she had started, without ever turning around!

We call such a universe a *closed universe.* A closed universe would be both infinite and finite, endless and limited, and it would have no edge.

If the universe does indeed curve in on itself, astronomers tell us that the expansion of the universe will eventually end, and the universe will collapse. The Big Bang will reverse itself, and all of the galaxies will be concentrated into a single point once again. And then another Big Bang may happen, creating a new universe, just like this one—or completely different.

Maybe there have been other universes before this one. And maybe there will be others after it, universe after universe, for the rest of time!

EPILOGUE

UNANSWERED QUESTIONS

What a long way we have come from the simple villager looking up at the sky! How our model of the universe has changed!

And yet it is still possible to look up at the sky and feel the same wonder that villager must have felt thousands of years ago. Today we know that the sky is not a dome and that the stars are not lanterns and that the whole show is not run by gods. But we know about neutron stars and black holes and quasars, and these things are more wonderful still.

The history of astronomy is a history of the painstaking gathering of evidence, which is used to construct a model of a universe that we can see only part of, from a great distance. But as our tools for gathering that evidence have improved, so has the speed with which that evidence can be gathered. As astronomers have progressed from the naked eye to the telescope to the radio telescope, our knowledge of the universe has changed at an ever faster rate.

Is our model of the universe complete? By no means. The sky is still full of unanswered questions, and perhaps the most important questions have not yet been asked. In recent years, astronomers have gained an even more powerful tool for the study of the universe: the space probe. Rocket-launched probes such as Voyager and Mariner have actually visited the planets and their

moons and sent back photographs of their surfaces. Astronauts have walked on Earth's moon and brought back moondust to be studied under the scientist's microscope. We have seen volcanoes on the surface of Mars and on a moon of Jupiter. We have seen unexpected rings around the planet Jupiter and dust storms on Mars. No life has been discovered on other planets, though scientists have not yet given up hope. But even without the discovery of life elsewhere, the solar system has already proved to be filled with wonders indeed.

And what of the future? There are plans to launch an optical telescope—that is, a visible-light telescope—into orbit around Earth. This project was scheduled for the end of 1986 but has been postponed indefinitely by the tragic accident to the Space Shuttle, which was to launch it. The Edwin Hubble Space Telescope, as it is called, will give astronomers an unprecedented view of the universe, because it will be free from the distortion of Earth's atmosphere. It will provide us with pictures of the planets almost as good as those returned by space probes. It may unlock the secrets of quasars and photograph the accretion disks of black holes.

It may alter our model of the universe as severely as did the discoveries of Galileo and the theories of Newton and Einstein.

The history of astronomy is far from over. It may be just beginning!

The Hubble Space Telescope will provide astronomers with a clear view of the universe.

GLOSSARY

Accretion disk—the swirling cloud of hot matter surrounding and descending into a black hole.

Asteroids—small planetlike bodies orbiting the sun, most (though not all) of which are concentrated between the orbits of Mars and Jupiter.

Big Bang—the explosion that most scientists believe represented the beginning of the universe.

Black hole—a collapsed star that produces so much gravity that light cannot escape from it.

Cepheid variable—a star that changes brightness in a regular, rhythmic pattern.

Closed universe—a model of the universe in which expansion will eventually stop and the universe will collapse.

Electromagnetic radiation—a spectrum of radiation that includes visible light, radio waves, x rays, gamma rays, and several other forms of radiation.

Electromagnetic spectrum—the full range of wavelengths of electromagnetic radiation, which include all the forms of electromagnetic radiation such as visible light and radio waves.

Ellipse—a shape similar to a circle, but which can be more stretched out in one direction; a circle is one kind of ellipse.

Epicycles—an imaginary "orbit within an orbit" that ancient astronomers believed explained the peculiar motion of the planets as viewed from Earth.

Expanding universe—a model of the universe, generally accepted as valid by modern astronomers, in which the universe is continually expanding outward from some unknown center, probably as the result of a long-ago explosion we call the Big Bang.

Geocentric Universe—a model of the universe, long held by ancient astronomers, in which all of the stars and planets, including the sun, orbit around the Earth.

Globular clusters—dense globe-shaped clusters of stars.

Gravity—a property, common to all objects, that attract other objects.

Heliocentric universe—a model of the universe in which the sun is at the center of the universe and everything else revolves around it.

Hydrogen fusion—a process by which atoms of the element hydrogen break apart, fuse together, and form atoms of the element helium, giving off large amounts of energy in the process.

Model—a way of looking at the universe, adopted by scientists to explain their observations and to help them make new observations.

Nebulae—clouds of gas and dust in outer space; the term is sometimes used incorrectly to describe galaxies, which are masses of stars that look "nebulous" when viewed through an optical telescope.

Neutron star—a very dense collapsed star made up entirely of the particles called *neutrons.*

Nova—an exploding star; literally, a "new star," since novae are often visible from Earth only when they explode.

Observational astronomer—an astronomer who observes phenomena in the heavens through instruments such as optical telescopes and radio telescopes.

Olbers' paradox—the observation that the universe cannot be filled with an infinite number of stars because the night sky could not be dark if it were.

Oort cloud—a halo of ice at the very edge of the solar system believed by many astronomers to be the source of comets.

Orbits—elliptical paths taken by objects in space moving perpetually around other objects, such as the moon around Earth or Earth around the sun.

Parallax—the apparent change in position of an object against a distant background when viewed from two different positions.

Planetesimals—miniature planets; early term for asteroids.

Pulsating star (pulsar)—object in space producing rhythmic electromagnetic signals detectable by radio telescopes; generally agreed to be a rotating neutron star.

Radio astronomy—the science of studying objects in space through the radio waves that they produce.

Radio telescope—telescope designed to detect radio waves from outer space.

Red shift—a change in the nature of the light produced by an object moving away from the viewer; a ''stretching out'' of the light waves.

Retrograde motion—an apparent reversal in the motion of a planet through Earth's sky.

Satellite—an object in orbit around another object, such as the moon around Earth.

Spectrum—the full range of wavelengths observable in a type of radiation, such as electomagnetic radiation (which includes all the colors of visible light, plus the full range of radio waves).

Supernova—the explosion of a large star at the end of its active life.

Telescope—instrument used by astronomers to study objects in outer space; optical telescopes are used to study light from the stars and include refracting telescopes, which have two

lenses placed at opposite ends of a tube, and reflecting telescopes, which have a mirror and a lens placed in and around
a tube; other types of telescopes include radio telescopes,
which are used to study radio waves, gamma ray telescopes,
and X-ray telescopes.

Theoretical astronomer—an astronomer who devises theories
based on the observations of an observational astronomer.

White dwarf—a dense, collapsed star, resulting from a supernova explosion.

INDEX